~A BINGO BOOK~

West Virginia Bingo Book

COMPLETE BINGO GAME IN A BOOK

Written By Rebecca Stark

ISBN 978-0-87386-541-8

© 2016 Barbara M. Peller

Educational Books 'n' Bingo

Printed in the U.S.A.

DIRECTIONS

INCLUDED:

List of Terms

Templates for Additional Terms and Clues

2 Clues per Term

30 Unique Bingo Cards

Markers

1. **Either cut apart the book or make copies of ALL the sheets. You might want to make an extra copy of the clue sheets to use for introduction and review. Keep the sheets in an envelope for easy reuse.**

2. Cut apart the call cards with terms and clues.

3. Pass out one bingo card per student. There are enough for a class of 30.

4. Pass out markers. You may cut apart the markers included in this book or use any other small items of your choice.

5. Decide whether or not you will require the entire card to be filled. Requiring the entire card to be filled provides a better review. However, if you have a short time to fill, you may prefer to have them do the just the border or some other format. Tell the class before you begin what is required.

6. There are 50 terms. Read the list before you begin. If there are any terms that have not been covered in class, you may want to read to the students the term and clues before you begin.

7. There is a blank space in the middle of each card. You can instruct the students to use it as a free space or you can write in answers to cover terms not included. Of course, in this case you would create your own clues. (Templates provided.)

8. Shuffle the cards and place them in a pile. Two or three clues are provided for each term. If you plan to play the game with the same group more than once, you might want to choose a different clue for each game. If not, you may choose to use more than one clue.

9. Be sure to keep the cards you have used for the present game in a separate pile. When a student calls, "Bingo," he or she will have to verify that the correct answers are on his or her card AND that the markers were placed in response to the proper questions. Pull out the cards that are on the student's card keeping them in the order they were used in the game. Read each clue as it was given and ask the student to identify the correct answer from his or her card.

10. If the student has the correct answers on the card AND has shown that they were marked in response to the *correct questions,* then that student is the winner and the game is over. If the student does not have the correct answers on the card OR he or she marked the answers in response to *the wrong questions,* then the game continues until there is a proper winner.

11. If you want to play again, reshuffle the cards and begin again.

Have fun!

TERMS INCLUDED

Adena Indians

Allegheny

Appalachian Plateau

Appalachian Ridge and Valley

Apple

Big Laurel

Black Bear(s)

Border

Brook Trout

Pearl S. Buck

Cardinal(s)

Carnifex Ferry

Chalcedony

Charleston

Climate

Coal

County (-ies)

Crop(s)

Droop Mountain

Executive Branch

Flag

Fort Henry

Harpers Ferry

Hatfield–McCoy

Honeybee

Huntington

Industries

Stonewall Jackson

Judicial Branch

Lakes

Legislative Branch

Livestock

Monongahela

Morgantown

Motto

Mountain State

New-Kanawha River

New River Gorge

Panhandle

Prickett's Fort

Quarter

River(s)

Seal

Shenandoah

Song(s)

Spruce Knob

Sugar Maple

Timber Rattlesnake(s)

Virginia

Wheeling

Additional Terms

Choose as many additional terms as you would like and write them in the
squares. Repeat each as desired.
Cut out the squares and randomly distribute them to the class.
Instruct the students to place their square on the center space of their card.

Clues for Additional Terms

Write two clues for each of your additional terms.

_____	_____
1.	1.
2.	2.
_____	_____
1.	1.
2.	2.
_____	_____
1.	1.
2.	2.

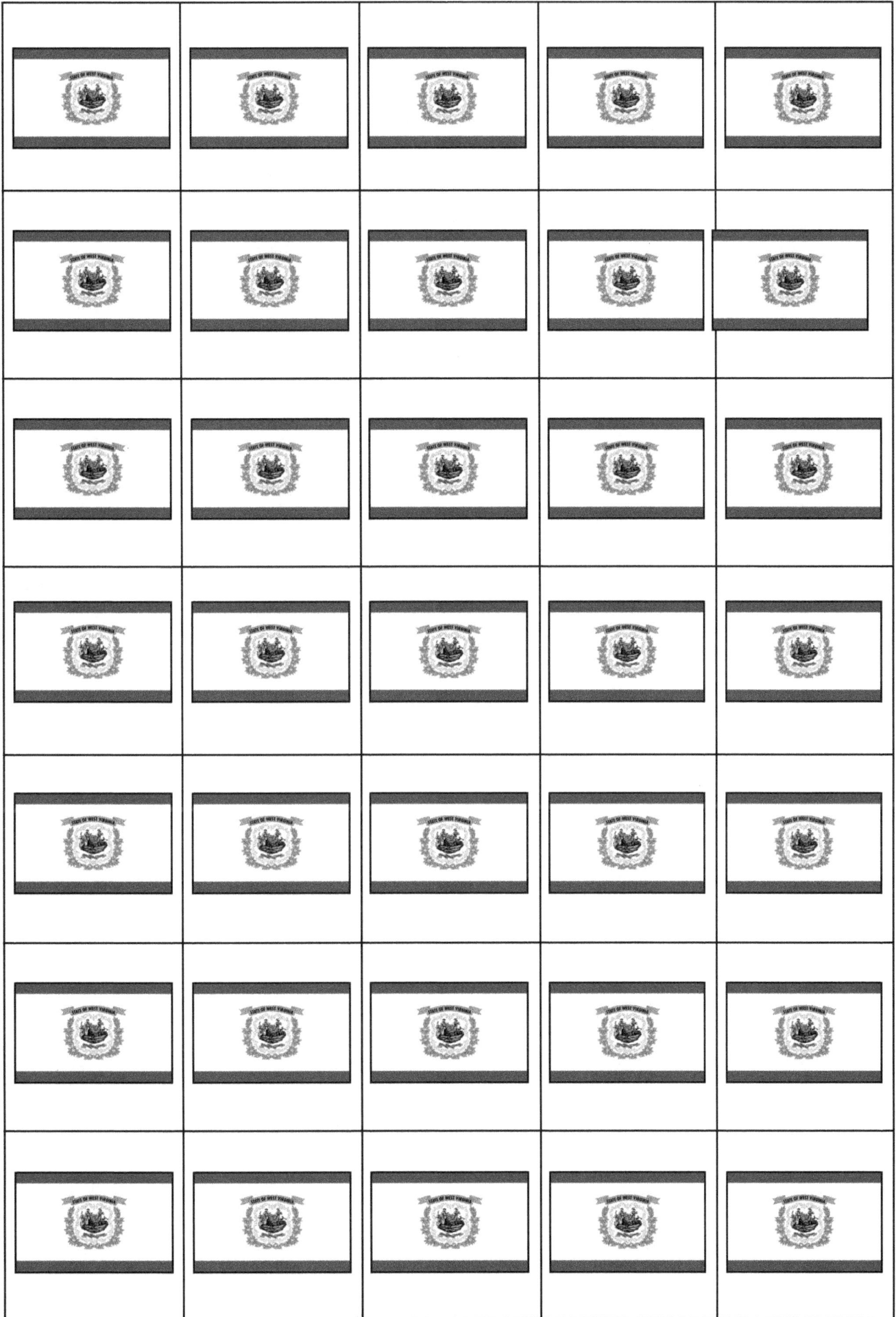

Adena Indians
1. West Virginia's earliest inhabitants were the mound-building ___.
2. The burial mounds of the ___ include the Grave Creek Mound, the largest earth mound east of the Mississippi River.

Allegheny
1. The ___ Mountains are part of the Appalachian Mountain Range.
2. The ___ Front is where the rugged mountains of the east meet the rolling terrain of the Appalachian Plateau.

Appalachian Plateau
1. The Appalachian ___ is west of the Appalachian Ridge and Valley. It covers the western 5/6 of the state.
2. The ___, which covers most of the western part of the state, is characterized by flat-topped highlands and rounded hills.

Appalachian Ridge and Valley
1. The Allegheny and Blue Ridge Mountain ranges in eastern West Virginia are part of the ___ Region.
2. The ___ region covers the eastern 1/6 of the state. It is characterized by long, narrow chains of mountains with valleys separating the ridges.

Apple
1. The golden delicious ___ is the state fruit.
2. The golden delicious ___ is native to West Virginia. It was discovered by Anderson Mullins in Clay County in 1905.

Big Laurel
1. ___ is the official state flower. It is a shrub of the heath family.
2. The scientific name of the ___ is *Rhododendron maximum;* it is the state flower.

Black Bear(s)
1. The ___ is the state animal.
2. The habitat of the ___ is mostly in the eastern mountain region. Despite their name, ___ show a great deal of variation in color.

Border
1. Ohio, Pennsylvania, Maryland, Virginia, and Kentucky ___ West Virginia.
2. During the Civil War, West Virginia was considered a ___ state.

Brook Trout
1. The ___ is the state fish.
2. ___ thrive in the cold, pure mountain streams of West Virginia.

Pearl S. Buck
1. This author is best known for her novel *The Good Earth.*
2. The home in Pocahontas County where this Nobel Prize-winning author was born in 1892 is now a National Historic Site.

West Virginia Bingo

Cardinal(s) 1. The state bird is the ___. 2. Male ___ are a brilliant scarlet red; females are a buffy brown with reddish wings.	**Carnifex Ferry** 1. The Confederates were defeated at the Battle at ___ on September 10, 1861. This made the movement toward statehood easier since the Confederates would not be able to interfere. 2. ___ Battlefield State Park is an important Civil War battle site.
Chalcedony 1. ___ is the state gemstone. 2. ___ is a translucent variety of quartz.	**Charleston** 1. ___ is the capital and largest city in West Virginia. It is in the Metro Valley region. 2. ___ was named after Charles Clendenin, a Revolutionary War soldier and owner of the land on which the settlement was built.
Climate 1. Most of the state has a humid continental climate ___, with hot summers and cool to cold winters. 2. Parts of the state have a humid subtropical ___, including some lower elevations in the southwest and parts of the Eastern Panhandle.	**Coal** 1. About 75% of West Virginia's mining income comes from ___. West Virginia is the nation's second largest producer of ___. 2. ___ is found in 53 of the 55 counties. Bituminous ___ is the official state rock.
County (-ies) 1. There are 55 ___ in West Virginia. 2. Charleston is in Kanawha ___.	**Crop(s)** 2. Hay, apples, corn for grain, soybeans and tobacco are important ___. **2.** Hay is the most important ___; it is needed to feed the livestock.
Droop Mountain 1. Battles were fought at ___ during the French and Indian War, Pontiac's War, Dunmore's War, the Revolutionary War, and the Civil War. 2. The last significant Civil War battle in West Virginia took place November 6, 1863, at ___ in the Greenbrier River Valley. West Virginia Bingo	**Executive Branch** 1. The ___ of government includes the governor, the secretary of state, the attorney general, the commissioner of agriculture, the auditor, and the treasurer. 2. The governor is head of the ___. The present-day governor is [fill in]. © Barbara M. Peller

Flag
1. The state ___ depicts the coat of arms on a white background. The ___ is bordered in blue.
2. Big laurel, the state flower, surrounds the coat of arms on the state ___.

Fort Henry
1. ___ was built to protect settlers on the frontier during Lord Dunmore's War in 1774. It was built on the site of present-day Wheeling.
2. Elizabeth Zane volunteered to retrieve powder from the Zane homestead during the 1782 siege of ___ by the British. She was fired upon but uninjured.

Harpers Ferry
1. ___ is at the confluence of the Potomac and Shenandoah rivers where Maryland, Virginia, and West Virginia meet. It is the easternmost town in West Virginia.
2. ___ is best known for John Brown's raid on the Armory in 1859.

Hatfield–McCoy
1. The ___ feud involved two families of the West Virginia–Kentucky area along the Tug Fork of the Big Sandy River.
2. The first event in this decades-long feud was the 1865 murder of Asa Harmon McCoy, brother of Randolph McCoy.

Honeybee
1. The ___ is the official state insect. The monarch is the official state butterfly.
2. The ___ is an official symbol in 17 states, probably because it plays such an important role in agriculture.

Huntington
1. ___ is the second largest city in West Virginia. Most of the city is in Cabell County.
2. ___ was created as a railroad town. It was named for the man who built it as the western terminus for the Chesapeake and Ohio Railway.

Industries
1. Important ___ include coal mining, livestock, chemical manufacturing, glass products, and tourism.
2. Forestry and timber production are also important ___.

Thomas Jonathan Jackson
1. This Confederate general was born in Clarksburg and grew up in Jackson's Mill. His nickname was "Stonewall."
2. He was first given the nickname "Stonewall" at the Battle of Bull Run by Brigadier-General Barnard E. Bee.

Judicial Branch
1. The ___ interprets what our laws mean and makes decisions about the laws and those who break them.
2. The ___ is made up of several courts, the highest of which is the state Supreme Court of Appeals.

Lakes
1. Tygart and Bluestone are two ___ in West Virginia.
2. Braxton, Clay, Lewis, Nicholas, Upshur, and Webster counties are in the Mountain ___ Region in the center of the state.

Legislative Branch
1. The General Assembly is the ___ of state government; it comprises the Senate and the House of Representatives.
2. The ___ makes the laws.

Livestock
1. More than 80% of West Virginia's agricultural production is in ___ products.
2. The most important ___ products are broilers, or young chickens, and beef cattle and calves. Chicken eggs, dairy products, and turkeys are other ___ products.

Monongahela
1. ___ silt loam is the state soil.
2. The name of this state soil is derived from a Native American word meaning "high banks or bluffs, breaking off and falling down in places."

Morgantown
1. Situated along the banks of the Monongahela River, ___ is home to West Virginia University.
2. ___ is known for its unique personal rapid transit system. Its vehicles resemble miniature buses.

Motto
1. In English the state ___ is "Mountaineers are always free."
2. In Latin the state ___ is *Montani Semper Liberi."*

Mountain State
1. West Virginia's nickname is the ___.
2. The state is nicknamed the ___; it is the only state to lie completely within a mountain range.

New-Kanawha River
1. Most Native America tribes identified these two rivers ___ as being one river. So did many early explorers.
2. Below the mouth of Gauley River, the ___ is called the Kanawha River; above the Gauley, it is called the New River.

New River Gorge
1. The ___ Bridge is depicted on the state quarter.
2. At 3,030 feet long and 69 feet wide, the ___ Bridge is the second highest bridge in the United States.

Panhandle
1. The land that extends eastward between Maryland and Virginia is referred to as the Eastern ___.
2. The strip of land that extends northward between Ohio and Pennsylvania is referred to as the Northern ___.

Prickett's Fort
1. ___ was built at the confluence of Prickett's Creek and the Monongahela River in 1774. Colonists took refuge at ___ for protection.
2. ___ State Park is north of Fairmont. Re-enactors include blacksmiths, spinners, and weavers. They also demonstrate 18th-century firearm manufacturing.

West Virginia Bingo

Quarter 1. West Virginia's state ___ features the New River Gorge Bridge. 2. West Virginia's state ___ was the 35th to be issued because West Virginia was the 35th state to be admitted into the Union.	**River(s)** 1. The Ohio, the Kanawha, the Big Sandy, the Potomac, and the Greenbrier are ___ in West Virginia. 2. The Big Sandy ___ forms part of the boundary between Kentucky and West Virginia.
Seal 1. The two men on the state coat of arms and the Great ___ represent mining and agriculture. 2. Etched in the boulder in the center of the Great ___ is the date of West Virginia's entrance into the Union.	**Shenandoah** 1. The Great Appalachian Valley is called the ___ Valley in Virginia and West Virginia. 2. The ___ Valley includes two counties in West Virginia: Berkeley County and Jefferson County.
Song(s) 1. "West Virginia, My Home Sweet Home," "The West Virginia Hills," and "This is My West Virginia" are official state ___. 2. Many consider John Denver's "Country Roads" the state's unofficial anthem, but it is not an official state ___.	**Spruce Knob** 1. At 4,863 feet above sea level, ___ is the highest point in the state. 2. The summit of Spruce Mountain, the highest peak in the Allegheny Mountains, is called ___.
Sugar Maple 1. The ___ is the state tree. Sap from its trunk is used to make maple syrup. 2. The wood of this hardwood tree is excellent for furniture.	**Timber Rattlesnake(s)** 1. The ___ is the state reptile. 2. These poisonous reptiles are commonly found in deciduous forests in rugged terrain.
Virginia 1. West Virginia seceded from ___ because it did not want to secede from the Union. 2. West Virginia became the 35th state when it seceded from ___ and joined the Union on June 20, 1863. West Virginia Bingo	**Wheeling** 1. ___ was the first capital of West Virginia. 2. ___ is on the Ohio River in the Northern Panhandle. It was the first capital of West Virginia.

West Virginia Bingo

Panhandle	Adena Indians	Appalachian Plateau	Droop Mountain	Apple
County (-ies)	Allegheny	Timber Rattlesnake(s)	Lakes	River(s)
Sugar Maple	Judicial Branch		Motto	Virginia
Quarter	New-Kanawha River	Spruce Knob	Stonewall Jackson	Livestock
Morgantown	Fort Henry	Charleston	Shenandoah	Huntington

West Virginia Bingo

Quarter	Sugar Maple	Hatfield–McCoy	Prickett's Fort	Honeybee
Livestock	Climate	Black Bear(s)	New-Kanawha River	Monongahela
Brook Trout	Fort Henry		Harpers Ferry	Apple
Mountain State	New River Gorge	Judicial Branch	Wheeling	Spruce Knob
River(s)	Timber Rattlesnake(s)	Charleston	County (-ies)	Shenandoah

West Virginia Bingo

Fort Henry	Spruce Knob	Climate	Stonewall Jackson	Sugar Maple
Livestock	Allegheny	Border	Adena Indians	Flag
New-Kanawha River	Timber Rattlesnake(s)		Monongahela	Appalachian Ridge and Valley
Judicial Branch	Brook Trout	Morgantown	Mountain State	Hatfield–McCoy
Shenandoah	Cardinal(s)	Charleston	Wheeling	Honeybee

West Virginia Bingo

Judicial Branch	Monongahela	Appalachian Plateau	Cardinal(s)	Honeybee
Legislative Branch	Big Laurel	Adena Indians	Prickett's Fort	Sugar Maple
Motto	Mountain State		Huntington	Droop Mountain
Spruce Knob	Allegheny	Timber Rattlesnake(s)	Charleston	Black Bear(s)
Carnifex Ferry	River(s)	Pearl S. Buck	Shenandoah	Virginia

West Virginia Bingo

River(s)	Apple	New-Kanawha River	Black Bear(s)	Cardinal(s)
Legislative Branch	Spruce Knob	Border	Harpers Ferry	Allegheny
Appalachian Plateau	Virginia		Lakes	Executive Branch
Huntington	Honeybee	Panhandle	Wheeling	Chalcedony
Climate	Charleston	Sugar Maple	Judicial Branch	Motto

West Virginia Bingo

Appalachian Ridge and Valley	Monongahela	Hatfield–McCoy	Honeybee	Virginia
Stonewall Jackson	New-Kanawha River	Chalcedony	Adena Indians	Sugar Maple
Prickett's Fort	Carnifex Ferry		Big Laurel	Harpers Ferry
Charleston	Morgantown	Wheeling	Pearl S. Buck	Appalachian Plateau
Livestock	Black Bear(s)	Panhandle	Motto	Coal

West Virginia Bingo

Panhandle	Monongahela	Executive Branch	Spruce Knob	Climate
Livestock	Honeybee	Fort Henry	Allegheny	Legislative Branch
Virginia	Droop Mountain		Harpers Ferry	Big Laurel
Judicial Branch	Mountain State	Border	Quarter	Brook Trout
Charleston	Cardinal(s)	Wheeling	Pearl S. Buck	Appalachian Ridge and Valley

West Virginia Bingo

Motto	Monongahela	Crop(s)	Stonewall Jackson	Big Laurel
Legislative Branch	Appalachian Plateau	Prickett's Fort	Virginia	Black Bear(s)
Coal	Cardinal(s)		Honeybee	Apple
Shenandoah	Judicial Branch	Quarter	Carnifex Ferry	Mountain State
Timber Rattlesnake(s)	Charleston	Pearl S. Buck	New-Kanawha River	Livestock

West Virginia Bingo

Harpers Ferry	Climate	Fort Henry	Coal	Cardinal(s)
Carnifex Ferry	Honeybee	Motto	New-Kanawha River	Monongahela
Flag	Panhandle		Allegheny	Crop(s)
Chalcedony	Apple	Morgantown	Lakes	Executive Branch
Mountain State	Wheeling	Border	Quarter	Huntington

West Virginia Bingo: Card No. 9

West Virginia Bingo

Quarter	Stonewall Jackson	Big Laurel	Prickett's Fort	Coal
Virginia	Black Bear(s)	Adena Indians	Allegheny	Honeybee
Cardinal(s)	Monongahela		Droop Mountain	Brook Trout
Morgantown	Huntington	Chalcedony	Wheeling	Flag
Border	Livestock	Hatfield–McCoy	River(s)	Motto

West Virginia Bingo: Card No. 10

West Virginia Bingo

Appalachian Ridge and Valley	Monongahela	New-Kanawha River	Chalcedony	Livestock
Crop(s)	Flag	Lakes	Harpers Ferry	Adena Indians
Legislative Branch	Honeybee		Hatfield–McCoy	Fort Henry
Border	Sugar Maple	Wheeling	Cardinal(s)	Quarter
Carnifex Ferry	Charleston	Panhandle	Pearl S. Buck	Climate

West Virginia Bingo

Climate	Apple	Flag	Stonewall Jackson	Harpers Ferry
Fort Henry	Livestock	Appalachian Plateau	Pearl S. Buck	Allegheny
Panhandle	Executive Branch		Virginia	Prickett's Fort
Charleston	Mountain State	Honeybee	Quarter	Legislative Branch
Monongahela	Crop(s)	Cardinal(s)	Carnifex Ferry	Black Bear(s)

West Virginia Bingo: Card No. 12

West Virginia Bingo

Chalcedony	Apple	Appalachian Ridge and Valley	Flag	Virginia
Appalachian Plateau	Crop(s)	Honeybee	Harpers Ferry	Brook Trout
Stonewall Jackson	Black Bear(s)		Fort Henry	Executive Branch
Motto	Wheeling	Big Laurel	Cardinal(s)	Quarter
Charleston	Huntington	Pearl S. Buck	Panhandle	Lakes

West Virginia Bingo

County (-ies)	Honeybee	New-Kanawha River	Harpers Ferry	Carnifex Ferry
Black Bear(s)	Panhandle	Flag	Allegheny	Monongahela
Chalcedony	Droop Mountain		Hatfield–McCoy	Border
Huntington	Wheeling	Cardinal(s)	Big Laurel	Appalachian Ridge and Valley
Charleston	Prickett's Fort	Brook Trout	Livestock	Motto

West Virginia Bingo: Card No. 14

West Virginia Bingo

Lakes	Harpers Ferry	New-Kanawha River	Climate	Stonewall Jackson
Appalachian Ridge and Valley	Hatfield–McCoy	Adena Indians	Appalachian Plateau	Carnifex Ferry
Virginia	Panhandle		Sugar Maple	Monongahela
Charleston	Flag	Crop(s)	Wheeling	Chalcedony
Livestock	Mountain State	Pearl S. Buck	Coal	Fort Henry

West Virginia
Bingo

West Virginia Bingo

Schoenian Indians	Climate	New Kanawha River	Rivers	Lakes
Conflex Ferry	Appalachian Plateau	Mound Indians	Senator McCoy	Appalachian Ridge and Valley
Monongahela	Sugar Maple		Panhandle	Virginia
Chalcedony	Wheeling	Crop(s)	Flag	Charleston
Fort Henry	Coal	Pearl S. Buck	Mountain State	Livestock

West Virginia Bingo

Big Laurel	Flag	Crop(s)	Coal	New River Gorge
Prickett's Fort	Brook Trout	Executive Branch	Legislative Branch	Droop Mountain
Chalcedony	Apple		Virginia	Fort Henry
Judicial Branch	Black Bear(s)	Charleston	Lakes	Quarter
Carnifex Ferry	Song(s)	Pearl S. Buck	Mountain State	Monongahela

West Virginia Bingo

Border	Seal	Industries	Flag	County (-ies)
Lakes	Carnifex Ferry	Wheeling	Droop Mountain	Executive Branch
Harpers Ferry	Motto		Song(s)	Crop(s)
Huntington	Livestock	Quarter	New-Kanawha River	Brook Trout
Morgantown	Chalcedony	Climate	Stonewall Jackson	Apple

West Virginia Bingo

Coal	Cardinal(s)	Black Bear(s)	Chalcedony	Prickett's Fort
Monongahela	Border	Morgantown	Virginia	Carnifex Ferry
Harpers Ferry	Brook Trout		Industries	Appalachian Plateau
Apple	Adena Indians	Wheeling	Quarter	Hatfield–McCoy
Song(s)	Flag	New-Kanawha River	Seal	Appalachian Ridge and Valley

West Virginia Bingo

Virginia	Appalachian Ridge and Valley	Flag	Crop(s)	Quarter
Lakes	Stonewall Jackson	Monongahela	Climate	Droop Mountain
Seal	Cardinal(s)		Allegheny	Sugar Maple
Hatfield–McCoy	Song(s)	Morgantown	Mountain State	Industries
Appalachian Plateau	New River Gorge	Livestock	Motto	Pearl S. Buck

West Virginia Bingo

County (-ies)	Seal	Stonewall Jackson	Flag	Pearl S. Buck
Black Bear(s)	Fort Henry	Legislative Branch	Morgantown	Prickett's Fort
Apple	Executive Branch		Judicial Branch	Adena Indians
River(s)	Timber Rattlesnake(s)	Shenandoah	Mountain State	Song(s)
Spruce Knob	Motto	New River Gorge	Quarter	Industries

West Virginia Bingo

Lakes	Appalachian Ridge and Valley	Legislative Branch	Flag	River(s)
Apple	Industries	Big Laurel	Crop(s)	Panhandle
Brook Trout	Livestock		Seal	New-Kanawha River
Morgantown	Climate	Song(s)	Huntington	Motto
Judicial Branch	New River Gorge	Pearl S. Buck	Border	Mountain State

West Virginia Bingo

Coal	Hatfield–McCoy	Industries	Appalachian Plateau	Chalcedony
Prickett's Fort	Stonewall Jackson	Sugar Maple	Crop(s)	Allegheny
Black Bear(s)	Droop Mountain		Panhandle	Executive Branch
Song(s)	Huntington	Mountain State	Adena Indians	Legislative Branch
New River Gorge	Border	Seal	Brook Trout	Judicial Branch

West Virginia Bingo

Big Laurel	Seal	Climate	Appalachian Plateau	Pearl S. Buck
Appalachian Ridge and Valley	County (-ies)	Livestock	Lakes	Adena Indians
Hatfield–McCoy	Chalcedony		Shenandoah	Panhandle
Brook Trout	New River Gorge	Song(s)	Border	Mountain State
River(s)	Timber Rattlesnake(s)	Motto	Morgantown	Industries

West Virginia Bingo

Big Laurel	Motto	County (-ies)	Seal	Crop(s)
Industries	Pearl S. Buck	Legislative Branch	Prickett's Fort	Panhandle
Executive Branch	Coal		Chalcedony	Brook Trout
River(s)	Shenandoah	Song(s)	Border	Apple
Spruce Knob	Judicial Branch	New River Gorge	Stonewall Jackson	Timber Rattlesnake(s)

West Virginia Bingo

Judicial Branch	Legislative Branch	Seal	New-Kanawha River	Industries
Adena Indians	Apple	Lakes	Big Laurel	Allegheny
Huntington	Crop(s)		Shenandoah	Song(s)
Sugar Maple	River(s)	Timber Rattlesnake(s)	New River Gorge	Droop Mountain
Pearl S. Buck	County (-ies)	Black Bear(s)	Carnifex Ferry	Spruce Knob

West Virginia Bingo

Industries	Seal	Hatfield–McCoy	Prickett's Fort	Coal
Morgantown	Stonewall Jackson	Crop(s)	County (-ies)	Big Laurel
Huntington	Shenandoah		Droop Mountain	Judicial Branch
Border	Appalachian Plateau	River(s)	New River Gorge	Song(s)
Executive Branch	Carnifex Ferry	New-Kanawha River	Timber Rattlesnake(s)	Spruce Knob

West Virginia Bingo: Card No. 26

© Barbara M. Peller

West Virginia Bingo

West Virginia Bingo

Hatfield–McCoy	Black Bear(s)	Seal	County (-ies)	Fort Henry
River(s)	Shenandoah	Lakes	Song(s)	Allegheny
Wheeling	Timber Rattlesnake(s)		New River Gorge	Judicial Branch
Coal	Appalachian Ridge and Valley	Legislative Branch	Spruce Knob	Adena Indians
Carnifex Ferry	Droop Mountain	Industries	Sugar Maple	Executive Branch

West Virginia Bingo

Hatfield–McCoy	County (-ies)	Sugar Maple	Seal	Big Laurel
Fort Henry	Industries	Shenandoah	Prickett's Fort	Droop Mountain
Timber Rattlesnake(s)	Brook Trout		Executive Branch	Morgantown
Quarter	Coal	Livestock	New River Gorge	Song(s)
Appalachian Plateau	Harpers Ferry	Carnifex Ferry	Spruce Knob	River(s)

West Virginia Bingo: Card No. 28

© Barbara M. Peller

West Virginia Bingo

Industries	County (-ies)	Coal	Lakes	Harpers Ferry
Mountain State	Morgantown	Legislative Branch	Executive Branch	Sugar Maple
Huntington	Shenandoah		Allegheny	Seal
Fort Henry	River(s)	Honeybee	New River Gorge	Song(s)
Big Laurel	Crop(s)	Spruce Knob	Appalachian Ridge and Valley	Timber Rattlesnake(s)

West Virginia Bingo

Cardinal(s)	Seal	Prickett's Fort	Harpers Ferry	Song(s)
Adena Indians	County (-ies)	Hatfield–McCoy	Droop Mountain	Allegheny
Huntington	Chalcedony		Executive Branch	Legislative Branch
Spruce Knob	Appalachian Ridge and Valley	Appalachian Plateau	New River Gorge	Shenandoah
River(s)	Virginia	Timber Rattlesnake(s)	Industries	Sugar Maple

ABOUT BINGO BOOKS

These games are a great way to introduce or review a subject! Each game provides a comprehensive overview of the topic. (Math and Analogy Bingo Games provide skill practice as well!)

There are two or three clues for every term, and there are enough unique bingo sheets for 30 students!

Enjoy!

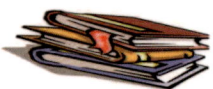

Educational Books 'n' Bingo

ISBN-13: 978-0873865418

9 780873 865418

~A BINGO BOOK~

Educational
Books 'n' Bingo
EBB4824

The Renaissance Bingo Book

COMPLETE BINGO GAME IN A BOOK

Madonna of the Magnificat
By Sandro Botticelli

Written By Rebecca Stark